THE

GOOD WILL

GUIDE

THE

GOOD WILL

GUIDE

PATRICIA C BYRON

S★B

Published in 2012 by:
Stellar★Books Publishing
Dunham Gatehouse
Charcoal Road
Bowdon,
Cheshire
WA14 4RY
Tel: 0161 928 8273

www.stellarbooks.co.uk

ISBN: 978-0956508911

First printed in 2012
Reprinted in 2013

A catalogue record for this book is available from the British Library

DISCLAIMER

This book relates to the law in England and Wales and whilst every effort has been made to ensure that it provides accurate information, it is not intended to be used as a source of legal advice. The author, editor, publisher, and retailer cannot be held liable to any person or entity with respect to any loss, expense or damage caused by, or allegedly caused by, any reliance upon the information contained in this book.

To Kit and Des
For the values you gave me

CONTENTS

Acknowledgments

Just how some scant notes written on a few sheets of paper have morphed into this work remains a mystery. With no thought other than attempting to assist a few I observed impartially, penned occasionally, pondered further, left it to prove and then scribbled some more. And so I deliver The Good Will Guide in the hope that it will assist you.

However, my simple notes would not be fit for consumption without the guidance and support I have received. Firstly, I must thank a diamond of a solicitor, Alison Armstrong of Armstrong Private Client, who has patiently offered guidance on the finer legal points. Without such counsel I could never have completed the task. Thanks, too, to the editor at Will and Probate Magazine, Oliver Waite of Oliver's Wills Ltd, for his valuable pointers. I would also like to thank the brilliant Presenter Media for allowing me to use the images within this book.

For the unconditional support given by my sister, Marie Nicholson, I give heartfelt thanks and, of course, to my uncle Joe Martin without whom life would be infinitely duller.

But it is with unending gratitude I thank my personal adviser, content editor, lawyer and friend, Tim Bullimore, who hears me out, argues the toss and reins in my rants.

Thank you all.

Regulation of Will-Writing

At the time of this book going to print, Will-writing is an unregulated profession. This essentially allows anyone to perform the act of writing a Will for another person.

There are currently some safeguards in place to protect consumers. For those professions which work under the auspices of a regulatory body there are prescribed codes of conduct which have to be adhered to but for those who do not have such constraints, principles may be less rigorous which may lead to compromised standards or even, in extreme cases, fraudulent activity.

Recent reports on Will-writing have found that systemic errors are being made across the board when drafting Wills. The reports have also found that levels of consumer protection between providers differed immensely and have recommended that all Will-writing should be regulated. This will only allow firms which work under a regulatory body to write Wills thus protecting consumers and enabling redress when things go wrong. These changes are expected in near future.

This book explains Will-writing in England and Wales as of 2012. Its content is applicable to anyone wishing to make a Will, but also to the millions of people who have already made a Will and wish to review it.

Preface

If you are looking for a weighty tome which probes and dissects the intricacies of trusts, includes templates of Wills using arcane, legalistic terminology and contains detailed tax avoidance schemes, this is not the book for you.

But if you want a clear, unbiased view of Will-making today from someone who regularly researches end-of-life issues from a lay person's perspective, who hears first-hand the apprehension which permeates the public on this important subject, and who considers not just the practical issues that need to be addressed but also looks at the holistic consequences of death, this book should prove useful and informative. There is also the very real chance it could save you money in the process.

In an ideal world we would all know a great deal more about how to get our affairs in order but, whilst we remain reluctant to openly discuss death, the media pay little relevant attention to it and some within Will-writing professions choose to use that apathy to their own advantage, the public will remain stymied.

This book is certainly not a panacea, but it is a start.

1

GOODWILL

♦

Whoever said that death and taxes are the greatest inevitabilities of our lives only got it half right. If you are rich enough, canny enough or even, at the other end of the spectrum, lazy enough you don't appear to have to pay taxes at all. But the other half of the statement is completely, undeniably and inescapably true. Death, the great leveller, will come to us all.

Given that we know the inevitable will happen, what is it that stops us from preparing for our demise and all its consequences? In the UK an astonishing two thirds of the population die without a Will in place, seemingly without any consideration for the trail of confusion and destruction that may be left in their wake. On the face of it we appear to be quite content to put our families through the emotional wringer. We purport to love them but we still leave them to tidy up the messiest of estates just because of our own dubious reservations and inertia. Why don't we take the necessary steps to ease their grief and support them at a time when it will be needed most? Surely we love them enough to do that?

For some there is a measure of superstition attached to making a Will: once it is written, it is a natural conclusion that the end is nigh. Yet the same irrational fear does not seem to apply when we insure the house against being burnt to the ground, or from being burgled, or the car being pranged, or insuring the pet against illness, or a holiday having to be cancelled. At vast expense, we annually pay sky-high premiums hoping none of these misfortunes will befall us. And yet we are still reluctant to properly prepare and make provision for something that is the greatest inevitability of our lives.

For others it may be that the burden of indecision weighs heavily. How to divide the estate? Who, in your mind, 'deserves' to receive anything? Are family members currently in or out of favour? Whilst these thoughts, and more, are relevant and understandable excuses for delaying the task, consider the alternative: you die without ever having made a Will at all. Then, through heedlessness, you will have unwittingly allowed your estate to be distributed in accordance with fixed legal rules and you will have had no say in how, and to whom, your assets are shared. If you have worked hard all of your life, perhaps denying yourself luxuries in order to save a nest-egg of sorts, it is difficult to fathom why you would not want a say in how that wealth is distributed after your death. Would you really prefer some faceless, nameless official to distribute your assets on your behalf without knowledge of, or concern for, your circumstances and your very personal relationships?

It could be that you are relying on the Rules of Intestacy - the legal term for deciding how your estate will be distributed if you die without a Will in place. You may be under the impression that your spouse will inherit everything anyway. You may be right, but you could be wrong. Is it worth the risk? Read on, as we will look at Intestacy in the next chapter.

Who should make a Will and when?

In legal terms, the minimum age is 18 although anyone on active military service can make a Will regardless of age. None of us knows the moment when our Will is going to be required so, in an ideal world, anyone with assets, property, business interests, or family responsibilities should attend to making one as a matter of course. Indeed, with current complex lifestyle choices, it has never been more important to.

Today, families are less structured than ever before; tenuous live-in partnerships, separations and divorce are no longer uncommon. Combine that with second and third marriages, adopted and step children, half-siblings and children born out of wedlock typifying the a modern day family, and it presents a cocktail of formal and informal associations, some or all of which could produce a claim on an estate. Without knowledge of the intricacies of law, it would be challenging for anyone to know precisely who could make a claim on their estate.

Against that backdrop, there are now more options than ever for making a Will but the uncomfortable truth is that, for many, the more simplified options just will not cater for the variances in their lives. Those with a complicated family structure will require a bespoke, tailored Will to accommodate their individual and specific needs. Someone with three ex-wives in tow, and children scattered liberally throughout the country, will have to make different provisions to those of a single, childless person with a cat.

Your Will could be the largest financial transaction of your life.

It is important to get it right!

Before we look at some of the Will-making options which are open to you, it is a sobering fact that in spite of recession we are, as a nation, wealthier today than previous generations. The wholesale increase in property prices has ensured that the sizes of our estates have grown and there is, therefore, more money than ever to bicker over. Add to that an ever growing awareness of our individual rights and the obvious consequence is that the amount of Wills that are contested is on the rise. It is of paramount importance, therefore, that your Will is robust enough to be able to withstand any challenge that could be made against it. If that isn't the main objective, one wonders why bother making a Will at all?

What is important is that you choose a method which is not just appropriate for the value of your estate but which also provides the level of support you wish to afford your loved ones. Do not only think about what is right for you: consider what is right for *them*. Remember, they will be without you to assist them.

Even if you have already made a Will, you may glean some useful information from the following pages which stirs you into reassessing the choices you once made. At the risk of stating the obvious, it is never too late to make a good decision and it would be better to revisit a poorly made Will than to leave it as it is.

◆

2

INTESTACY

♦

B efore you think about making a Will, let's look at what would happen if, for whatever reason, you die without ever having taken the time to make one. You will die what is called 'intestate' - that is, without a legally valid Will.

The Rules of Intestacy are complex but put very simply, if you die and have not made a Will, your estate will be distributed by the State in a way that is prescribed by law. This may or may not correspond with how you would have thought, or chosen, to distribute your assets. The people you wanted to inherit everything may receive nothing; the people you wanted to receive nothing may collect everything and between those two extremes are countless permutations depending on the size of your estate and the structure of your family. Further still, if you have no surviving blood relatives your estate may even end up with the Crown. So, as you can see, relying on the Rules of Intestacy to distribute your estate can, at best, be seen as precarious and at worst irresponsible.

As serious financial implications and the distribution of assets are brought to the fore it also increases the very real possibility of in-house conflict which is, undeniably, one of the worst and most calamitous consequences of death for a family to deal with. Grieving for the loss of a loved one is traumatic enough without the avoidable in-house wrangling which can accompany bereavement. Leaving your loved ones the gift of a supportive family at peace with itself is one of the greatest legacies anyone can bestow.

Leaving a good legacy

We often talk about leaving a legacy, referring to leaving a financial inheritance, but it is just as important to consider the wider implications of death. In the broader sense, your legacy also relates to how you will be remembered.

Did you leave the most extraordinary shambles which took your loved ones years of heartache and expense to resolve, or did you leave everything in apple pie order, thus supporting them even after you had shuffled off this mortal coil? Will your loved ones remember you as a steadfast brick, someone they could totally rely upon even after death, or as someone who left a trail of confusion and destruction which caused nothing but family rifts and disputes? In this sense, a poor legacy lives on and can affect your loved ones and even their children for, potentially, the rest of their lives so it is important that you protect the people you care about most. If you are prepared to look after them throughout your lifetime, why would you choose to be indifferent to what happens to them after your death?

If taking care of your loved ones isn't incentive enough, consider the financial implications of intestacy. You may wish to check the simple Intestacy Flow Chart to see how your loved ones would fare if you leave no valid Will. It may surprise you to learn that it is not always a foregone conclusion that your spouse will receive everything.

Intestacy Flow Chart

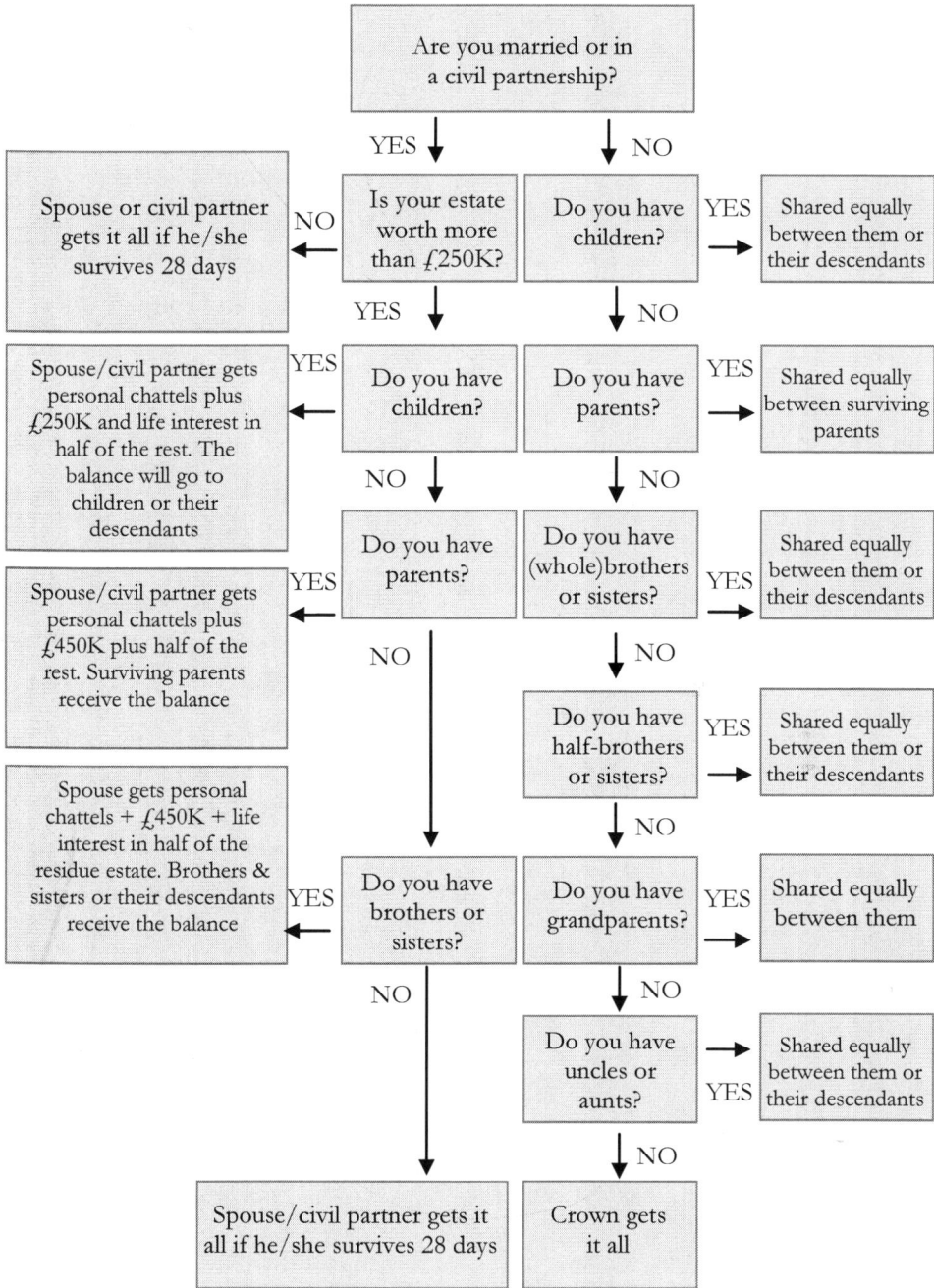

Are you married or in a civil partnership?

YES → Is your estate worth more than £250K?

NO → Do you have children?

Is your estate worth more than £250K?
- **NO** → Spouse or civil partner gets it all if he/she survives 28 days
- **YES** → Do you have children?

Do you have children? (under married, NO to £250K question)
- **YES** → Spouse/civil partner gets personal chattels plus £250K and life interest in half of the rest. The balance will go to children or their descendants
- **NO** → Do you have parents?

Do you have parents?
- **YES** → Spouse/civil partner gets personal chattels plus £450K plus half of the rest. Surviving parents receive the balance
- **NO** → Do you have brothers or sisters?

Do you have brothers or sisters?
- **YES** → Spouse gets personal chattels + £450K + life interest in half of the residue estate. Brothers & sisters or their descendants receive the balance
- **NO** → Spouse/civil partner gets it all if he/she survives 28 days

---

Do you have children? (under NO to married)
- **YES** → Shared equally between them or their descendants
- **NO** → Do you have parents?

Do you have parents?
- **YES** → Shared equally between surviving parents
- **NO** → Do you have (whole)brothers or sisters?

Do you have (whole)brothers or sisters?
- **YES** → Shared equally between them or their descendants
- **NO** → Do you have half-brothers or sisters?

Do you have half-brothers or sisters?
- **YES** → Shared equally between them or their descendants
- **NO** → Do you have grandparents?

Do you have grandparents?
- **YES** → Shared equally between them
- **NO** → Do you have uncles or aunts?

Do you have uncles or aunts?
- **YES** → Shared equally between them or their descendants
- **NO** → Crown gets it all

If you are married with children and living in England or Wales, the most your spouse would inherit outright is currently capped at £250,000. He or she would have the benefit of (but not the spending of) half of the remainder of the estate in what is termed 'life interest' which would ultimately go to your children on your spouse's death. Your children would inherit the rest. If they are under 18 years of age, the inheritance would be placed in a trust fund until they are adults.

An example:

> Let's assume your estate is worth £500,000. If you die intestate, your spouse will receive the maximum of £250,000 leaving £250,000 in the estate pot. He or she will have a life interest of half of the remainder, £125,000, which your children will inherit on your spouse's death. Your children will receive the remaining £125,000 once they are 18. In the interim, that £125,000 would be placed in a trust fund.

> Straightforward enough, but let's consider the not unlikely scenario where the bulk of your £500,000 estate is tied up in the family home, and your children are no longer minors but adults. Let's also assume that your spouse is not in a position, for whatever reason, to buy them out of their share of the property. But your children want, and are entitled to, their money. There have been instances where the children in such cases have demanded the surviving parent sell the family home so they can tap into their inheritance. Would you want this for your spouse? Don't think this doesn't happen.

Taking the same £500,000 estate, if you are married and have no children, your spouse will receive £450,000 and half of the residue, £25,000, and your parents, if still alive, will share the balance of £25,000. If they are deceased, your siblings will receive equal shares of the balance.

If you are unmarried and have no children and no blood relatives, the State will receive it all. It appears to be extreme, particularly when there are plenty of charities which would be more than grateful for a donation.

A few of the many incentives not to die intestate:

- If your estate is worth more than £325,000 you could end up paying IHT on anything above that figure at a rate of 40 percent. This could be avoided or reduced by seeking advice.

- If you are married or in a civil partnership, but have children from a previous marriage, they may not receive anything under the Rules of Intestacy. Your current spouse could have the strongest claim on your estate.

- If you are separated from your spouse, but not yet divorced, he/she will have a claim on your estate. This is particularly disconcerting if you had just won the lottery.
  (Note that divorce is recognised as being complete on decree absolute.)

- If you are living with someone but are not married to them, your partner could potentially be homeless as well as partner-less in the space of a few months after your death. The Rules of Intestacy does not automatically recognise cohabitants as having rights on a partner's estate although your partner could attempt to make a claim on your estate.

- If you have children or dependants, there may be uncertainty as to who should take care of them. You can appoint guardians in your Will.

- If you die intestate and have step children, they will have no automatic claim on your estate.

- If you want to leave a gift of money to a charity and you haven't made a Will, it will inherit nothing.

- If you want to leave a gift of money to friends but you haven't made a Will, they will inherit nothing.

- Conversely, if you don't want to leave money to certain individuals within your family and you die intestate, they may still inherit under the Rules of Intestacy.

- Given the complications your loved ones could face, they will be likely to instruct a law firm to tidy up matters so it will almost certainly prove to be a costly affair.

- In the broader sense, you will leave a poor legacy.

How to ensure none of these things happen? Make a Will.

◆

3

First Things First

◆

Before we start to examine your Will-making options it would be helpful for you to calculate the current value of your estate. This useful exercise will assist you in a number of ways: firstly, it will give you an indication of the funds you are working with which may, in turn, help you decide how you would like to distribute your estate. It will also show whether, in today's terms, your estate would be liable for Inheritance Tax (IHT) and finally, if you consult with a professional, you will have the figures to hand and give the impression that you are one financially-focussed savvy consumer.

First, make a list of your assets. Ensure that you include:

- Bank accounts

- Building society accounts

- Assurance policies
  (This is a policy which guarantees payment on death.)

- Insurance policies
  (These are policies which insure your life for a fixed term. Check the date when the term ends. The policy is worth nothing after that date.)

- Any annuity lump sum that may be payable on death

- Pension lump sums that may be payable on death

- Endowment policies
  (Use the amount payable on death, not the current value of the policy.)

- Stocks and shares

- Premium bonds

- Any business interests that are not covered by IHT relief. Seek professional advice if necessary.

- The sum total of your personal possessions, also known as chattels. Include high value items such as cars, jewellery, words of art, valuable collections and so on. The open market value should be used.

- The value of your property and/or your share of any property you jointly own with A. N. Other.
  (Note: if your property is owned in joint names, it is important that you take into account whether your property is owned as 'joint tenants' or as 'tenants in common'. The former will automatically pass to your spouse under survivorship rather than under your Will so is not considered part of your estate; the latter means that you each own a portion of the property so you can choose who you gift it to.)

If you have a nagging feeling that you may have misplaced an account visit My Lost Account, a free service which can assist you to track down mislaid accounts and investments.

Against the total of your assets, subtract:

- Outstanding loans

- Overdrafts

- Mortgages

- Credit card balances

- Any other debts

Once this has been done you will have the value of your estate and you can work out whether it would be liable for Inheritance Tax.

Inheritance Tax

At the time of this book being published, the IHT threshold is £325,000 (2012-2013) so if your estate is greater than this figure, or if you are married or in a civil partnership and together your assets are greater than £650,000 (2012-2013), your estate would be liable for IHT. The government has announced that these thresholds will remain the same until 2014/2015 but you should be aware that IHT rates and thresholds could increase or decrease in the future. Anything over and above these figures is currently charged at a rate of 40 percent. Alternatively, for those with philanthropic leanings, who wish to leave ten percent or more of their net estate to charity, there is the option of paying the reduced IHT rate of 36 percent.

An example of what, in the normal course of events, you could pay or avoid:

> Let us look at a £400,000 estate which will have an IHT allowance of £325,000. The remaining £75,000 would be subject to IHT and therefore taxed at a rate of 40 percent, so the tax man would take £30,000 (£75,000 x 40 divided by 100).

Alternatively, you could seek professional advice and see whether you could avoid paying some, or all of the £30,000. Having worked and saved for most of our lives, one would imagine that it would be a foregone conclusion that paying IHT would be an anathema but, due to apathy or a lack of awareness, members of the public appear to be content to pay it. With some forward planning it could, potentially, be avoided. It is your choice.

You should now be in a position to start making some decisions about how you would like to distribute your estate. Of course, we hope that this will not be the case for some considerable time, but you need to make your Will as if it would be required in the next six months. There will be plenty of time to review it in years to come when, or if, your circumstances change. Generally there are three choices of how you leave a gift in your Will: specific, pecuniary or residuary.

Specific gifts

A specific gift relates to a specific item that you wish to leave to a particular individual. Often these include high value items such as a car, a work of art, a piece of jewellery or a family heirloom. However, it is just as likely to refer to items of great sentimental importance which, although not financially valuable, could end up being the source of contention after bereavement. By making key decisions about such items now you could save your executors a lot of difficulties, and undue pressure, in deciding how to distribute them in the future.

In order to avoid misunderstandings, it is essential that there are detailed descriptions of any specific items included in a Will. This is particularly relevant when there is an item that may be classed as similar to another. For example, in order to avoid ambiguity, if you have two diamond rings, you may need to take photographs, supply valuations of each item and then state which item is to go to which beneficiary.

Pecuniary gifts

A pecuniary legacy is when you leave a set amount to a beneficiary; for example, "I leave 'A' the sum of ten thousand pounds". This fixed amount will not change no matter whether your estate increases or decreases over time. However you should be mindful that the spending power of any given pecuniary gift will diminish over time due to inflation. In order to ensure that the value of the gift is maintained in real terms, you have the choice of either making a point of regularly updating the pecuniary legacy by making changes to your Will or, alternatively, you can state when making your Will, that you wish the amount to be index-linked so that it will increase in line with inflation. Pecuniary gifts take priority and are paid before residuary gifts.

Residuary gifts

The residue is the amount of money which is left over once all the deceased's funeral costs, debts and any pecuniary gifts have been paid. You can then choose how you would wish the remaining pot to be distributed. Usually this is noted in percentage shares. For example, "I leave 'A' 20 percent, 'B' 40 percent" and so on until you reach 100 percent.

The amount that is left in the residual pot can increase or decrease over time. It will largely depend on the size of your estate and whether, for example, you choose to SKI, (Spend the Kids' Inheritance) whether you have care home fees or, on a more positive note, you have a Euro-millions win. The main advantage in leaving your beneficiaries residual gifts as opposed to pecuniary gifts is that it will ensure that the relative amount that anyone receives will remain in proportion with every other residuary beneficiary's legacy.

Making decisions

How you wish to distribute your estate is your decision and may take some considerable thought. Whether you wish to leave one son, Good Guy, the lion's share and virtually disown the other son, Bad Boy, is entirely your choice but you should be aware that there may be legal ramifications in doing so. Certain family members and dependants have rights to seek financial provision if they are either left out of or are not adequately provided for in a Will. Under the 1975 Inheritance Act it would appear that everyone has a moral obligation to look after a spouse, children or other dependants whom they have supported in some way for at least two years prior to their death. It certainly gives cause for thought. If this is an issue for you, it would be prudent to seek legal advice to determine the best way to provide for your dependents.

Testamentary Capacity

Choosing how you wish to distribute your estate also raises the issue of Testamentary Capacity; a legal term which describes your mental ability to make or alter a Will. This particularly important requirement verifies that not only were you of sound mind at the time of making your Will, but that you were fully aware of the decisions made and their implications. If your actions, for whatever reason, could be seen as confused or out of character, there is always the possibility that your Will could be challenged by someone who believes they have a claim, or a greater claim, on your estate. After all, a Will which seems to be perfectly reasonable to you may appear to be utterly deranged to another, (invariably because you have virtually disinherited them) so proving you were mentally stable when you made your Will is crucial, particularly if its content is likely to be seen as controversial.

As a nation we are living longer and are wealthier than ever but that gives rise to two things: it increases the chance of failing mental faculties and of there being more money to wrangle over in any given Will. So, as contestations of Wills increase, one of the first issues that will be raised will involve your Testamentary Capacity: were you of sound mind when you made your Will? It is at such times, and in these circumstances, that a professional witness, such as your doctor or a solicitor, could well prove to be invaluable as it is markedly more difficult to challenge a professional's assessment; without it, your Will is undeniably weakened. As we will see, some Will-making methods do not offer this assurance.

Pets

At this point those with pets may wish to consider what they would like to happen to them. It may be that there is a simple and natural progression of the pet(s) going to a family member but if that is not an option, you may wish to leave the pet in your Will to someone as a specific gift and make some kind of financial provision for the care of it. Alternatively, if you have no surviving relatives or friends able to take on the role, consider the RSPCA's scheme Home For Life or the highly regarded Cinnamon Trust. Both charities will take care of a pet for the rest of its life after the demise of its owner. They do require that a clause is inserted in your Will leaving the pet to the charity before they have the legal right to take on the ownership, and subsequent care, of him/her.

You are now ready to write your Will, so think about collating a list of your beneficiaries' names and addresses. Should you wish to donate to charity, check the charity's official name, address and registered charity number. You will need these details later. Let us now look at some Will-making options which are open to you.

Did You Know?

The first Inheritance Tax was implemented by Julius Caesar
Source: www.inheritanceissues.co.uk

♦

HMRC - the tax man - accrued a tidy £2.9 billion in Inheritance Tax
in the year 2011-2012. This is largely due to the public's indifference
to take steps to avoid it.
Source: HMRC

♦

4

DIY WILL KITS

◆

An over-the-counter DIY Will kit is one of the most convenient Wills you can buy, offering an unrivalled immediacy to the Will-making process. Retailing at around ten pounds in most high street stationers it is also, undoubtedly, the most inexpensive way of making a Will. However, whilst such a Will may be adequate in the simplest of cases, it is clearly not appropriate for all. For those who have estates of significant value with convoluted assets, trusts or complex family ties outside of the norm, the DIY Will is largely unsuitable.

The Society of Trust and Estate Practitioners (STEP), as the name suggests, is a world-wide professional body for practitioners in the fields of trusts, estates and legacies, which has collated many examples where the results of DIY Wills have been "disastrous".

Even if such a Will has been completed correctly, is legally sound and sails through Probate, the Will-maker (testator) may inadvertently drop clangers. For example, bequeathing all of your estate to your spouse may seem like a natural thing to do but, in certain circumstances, if your estate is worth more than the IHT threshold, it may not be most efficient way of to avoid paying tax. You should seek professional advice before you make such weighty decisions; it could save you and your loved ones a great deal of money.

Equally troubling, a DIY Will may have been written in such a way that proves to be extremely problematic for lay executors to administer. You may well have the best of intentions in leaving money to a charity but charities are obliged by law to maximise the amount of money they receive when named as a beneficiary in a Will. This can result in them being particularly forceful in challenging poorly drawn Wills or even, if the gift is a residual bequest, making the handling of the estate laborious for the lay executor. If you are of a mind to leave a gift of money to charity, and it is certainly not the intention to discourage you from doing so, it would be worth seeking professional advice to see which is the most efficient way of doing so.

The DIY Will form itself is not confusing; the Will kit includes instructions on how to complete the form plus examples and templates to follow, but that does not mean that mistakes are never made. In spite of best efforts made by the DIY Will kit publishers, there is still a catalogue of errors which are regularly made in the completion process. According to the Probate Office more DIY Wills fail than any other type of Will. This isn't due to the shortcomings of the Will kits but the testators who complete them. Unfortunately, if that should happen, a sorry mess can ensue leaving part, or potentially all, of the Will invalid.

Common mistakes made completing the DIY Will:

- The testator (Will-maker) fails to sign and date the Will correctly.

- The signing of the Will is not witnessed by two independent witnesses.

- The Will did not appoint executors.

- One or both of the two independent witnesses do not date the Will correctly.

- One of the witnesses is a beneficiary of the Will.

- One of the witnesses is a spouse of a beneficiary of the Will.

- Changes are made to the Will without them being signed and witnessed appropriately.

- The Will is never found because no one knew it existed.

- The Will is never found. It was destroyed by someone who didn't care for its content.

- The Will is found but is so damaged as to render it void.

Of course one could argue that some of these oversights apply to all Wills and indeed they do but having a professional oversee the exercise should minimise the risks.

If you have already written a DIY Will, take a look at it and check that you have correctly completed the form with the above points in mind.

Key points about DIY Will kits:

- They are inexpensive and convenient but not foolproof.

- They may be suitable for the simplest of Wills, but ONLY if completed correctly.

- No advice is given. Without the benefit of professional input you may make poor financial decisions which could cost your estate dearly.

- Without knowledge of the law, it may be poorly drafted leaving problems for your executors.

- Without having consulted with a professional, you will not have been assessed for Testamentary Capacity.

- If your Will is contentious, there are more chances of this type of Will being challenged. Your Will may not withstand the contest.

- According to the Probate Office, more DIY Wills are rejected at Probate than any other type of Will.

- If it is rejected any beneficiaries who aren't related to you will not receive their inheritance; beneficiaries who are may still receive under the Rules of Intestacy. Check the flow chart on page 7.

- If it is rejected the DIY Will exercise will almost certainly prove to be a false economy. Solicitors often make more out of putting these issues straight than drafting new Wills.

◆

5

ONLINE WILLS

◆

With the advent of the internet there is a growing trend in online Will-writing. Offered by Will-writers, law firms, charities and seemingly random organisations, there is an abundance of interactive Will templates which can cost anything from £25 to £100. In some cases there are optional, additional fees for the final drafts of Wills to be checked over by a qualified solicitor (or more likely, a paralegal) before the documents are sent out.

On the face of it, it would appear to be a simple, speedy and convenient way to make a Will: tick a few boxes, type your requirements into the computer and the Will templates will refine and sieve through your data to see whether you are a suitable candidate for an online Will. If your needs are different from the templates available, the service will not be appropriate either for you or the Will provider. So, if you have business interests, property abroad, if your estate is valued above the current IHT threshold or if your family structure is outside of the norm, this type of Will is unsuitable.

While completing the online form, you may even be asked whether you are of sound mind. As previously mentioned, having the mental capacity to make a Will is necessary if it is to be upheld. To what level ticking an online Will's box can verify one's mental faculties is a moot point.

It would be easy to assume that because you are making a Will, potentially via a law firm's website, the Will you end up with is going to be perfectly suited to your circumstances. It may not be. As with DIY Will kits, there is no consultation with a professional and no guidance offered so, whilst the online provider should produce a perfectly valid Will, it may not be the best possible, nor the most advantageous. Remember, merely producing a legally valid Will is not the end goal; producing one which effectively safeguards your assets and protects your loved ones in the future is.

A further cause for concern lies in the fact that there is no method of verifying who has completed the application. Anyone with access to a computer and the internet could draft a Will without the need for identification so there is an undeniable risk of fraud.

Finally, some online services have a default option by which the provider automatically appoints itself as an executor. One has to be particularly clued up to ensure you are not appointing the Will provider as a sole executor – a service for which, in due course, it will undoubtedly expect to be paid.

Key points to remember when considering an online Will:

- Inexpensive, typically ranging from £25 to £100.
- Even if the online Will is provided by a law firm, it may offer you a false sense of security. The Will may not be best suited to your circumstances.
- Without the presence of a professional, you will not be

assessed for Testamentary Capacity.

- There is the potential for fraud.

- Note the default option for some online Will providers to appoint themselves as an executor. If you have already made a Will this way, check to see if this is the case.

◆

Did You Know?

The oldest document that represents a Will was discovered by an archaeologist named Sir Flinders Petrie during an excavation of a tomb in Egypt. The tomb dated back to 2500 BC.

◆

Today, approximately 1.8 million Wills are prepared each year.
Source: The Legal Services Consumer Panel Report on Regulating Will Writing (July 2011)

◆

6

WILL-WRITERS

♦

Will-writers are individuals or firms who are in the business of writing Wills, usually at a seemingly economical price in a convenient setting. The cost of the Will is usually a fraction of what a solicitor would charge and, as the Will-writer often visits potential clients in their own homes, the testator is relieved from having to visit a law firm which, for some, can be an intimidating ordeal. The Will-writer therefore presents an undeniably attractive alternative.

Unfortunately Will-writing is currently an unregulated profession. Essentially, this allows anyone to set up a business and call himself a 'Will-writer' without any qualifications, training or professional indemnity insurance. According to the Law Society, the public is being exposed to "unqualified and uninsured Will-writers". Many solicitors have collated cases of people who have "turned to them for help after being left with what can only be described as nightmare Wills (written by) Will-writers, many of which are not worth the paper they are written on."

The Law Society may or may not be justified in tarring all Will-writers with the same brush, but what is undeniable is the inconsistent level of expertise within this sector. There are well qualified, competent Will-writers who offer a quality, bespoke service which is every bit as proficient as that of a solicitor; there are others who are considered to be 'qualified' having completed a three day training course. If you are unfamiliar with the issues which will be discussed and the terminology that will be used, would you be confident in your ability to tell the difference between the two?

Having a Will which is poorly drafted by an inadequately 'qualified' Will-writer is one thing; having a Will which has been written with the sole intention of lining the Will-writer's pocket is quite something else. As matters currently stand, there is nothing to stop scurrilous ne'er-do-wells setting themselves up as Will-writers, complete with a flashy website, copied logos and letter-headed paperwork and then preying on unsuspecting, vulnerable people. Such activity produces endless fodder for investigative journalism and sadly casts a slur on those decent Will-writing firms which offer a conscientious and valuable service. Whilst it is important to point out that this corruption relates to just a minority of Will-writers, it is necessary to highlight this rogue element if only to caution those who may have already, unwittingly, used such a Will-writer to make their Will.

A recent STEP report (entitled Cowboy Will Writing) highlighted incidences of Will-writing companies either going out of business or completely disappearing. Wills which had been prepared, paid for and supposedly safely stored by Will-writers, could not to be traced when testators died, causing chaos and heartache for their families. The report went on to find that some Will-writers levied surcharges for 'extras'. These included an annual fee for Will storage, additional fees for particular clauses and further review charges, all of which ensured the final bill often totalled more than ten times the advertised price. Some Will-making consultants fraudulently claimed to be as qualified as solicitors and had gone so far as to appoint themselves as executors to clients' Wills, which was highly lucrative for the consultant, but disastrous for the estates' beneficiaries. More worrying still, some estates suffered from large scale fraud and theft, through dishonest administration carried out by the Will-writing executor after the testator had died. Such activity makes for harrowing reading, not least as these illustrations have affected countless lives, with families suffering financial losses all at a time of profound personal grief.

Many Will-writers choose to wear other professional hats; along with writing Wills some are financial advisors who, amongst other things, sell mortgages, insurance and pensions. As financial advisors they, and the products and services they sell, are authorised and regulated by the Financial Services Authority. The FSA is an independent non-governmental body which regulates the financial services industry in the UK. It does not, however, regulate Wills nor offer any form of redress in connection with those written by financial advisors. So whilst these businesses and individuals may be reputable, reassuringly regulated and competent when it comes to selling you financial products, they may be no more qualified to write your Will than your postman.

Unfortunately there is no easy way to distinguish which Will-writers are reputable and which aren't but if you choose to go down the route of using a Will-writer, you should ensure that the firm or individual is a member of either the Institute of Professional Will Writers (IPW) or the Society of Will Writers. These are organisations which self-regulate and, according to their websites, have stringent membership criteria, proficiency standards, professional indemnity insurance and training for its members. IPW members have various consumer safeguards in place including arbitration via the Estate Planning Arbitration Scheme.

Key points when using a Will writing firm:

- Convenience: often these firms are prepared to visit you in your home but...

- Beware: that may lead to sharp selling practices and pressurised selling in your own home.

- Will-writers are self-regulated. That is, they police themselves.

- There is an inconsistency in Will-writers' expertise.

- Charges range from around £50 - £100 per Will but......

- Check for costly hidden charges most likely surrounding annual Will storage which can vary considerably.

- There may be further charges for additional clauses in a Will which can prove costly.

- Some firms may appoint themselves as executor of your Will.

- Remember, the FSA has nothing to do with Will writing.

- Check that the Will-writer has Professional Indemnity Insurance via the body they state they represent.

- The IPW has consumer safeguards in place via the Estate Planning Arbitration Scheme.

- According to the Legal Services Consumer Panel report 2011 around 10 percent of people making a Will use a Will-writer. The Office of Fair Trading report of 2010 suggests seven percent.

If you are in doubt and uncomfortable about using
a Will-writer, go to a solicitor

Sadly, and crucially, errors which are made in the process of writing any Will are usually only discovered after the death of the testator and on application for Probate, by which time it is too late to correct them.

If you have already made your Will using a DIY Will kit, an on-line Will, or via a Will-writer, it is strongly recommended that you get it checked by a solicitor or a member of STEP while you still have the ability to remedy any mistakes which may have been made.

◆

Did You Know?

Some Will-making rules are waived for members of the armed forces who are deployed on active military duty. For example:

- A Will can be made regardless of age.

- A Will can be made with the spoken word in place of a written Will (as long as the statement is made with the intention of it being a lasting Will)

- A Will which is written does not need to be witnessed.

Although Wills made using these rules have been found to be legal even many years later, it would be prudent to make a fresh Will once the person has returned to civilian life.

7

BANKS

♦

When it comes to Wills banks are seemingly happy to play the long game, sometimes waiting years before their profit is realised. By effectively offering a sprat to catch a mackerel, customers, usually with qualifying prestige accounts, are baited by a seemingly attractive low cost, or even no cost, Will only for the bank to appoint itself as an executor in the small print thus committing the customer to the bank's expensive Probate administration services in the future. Often the fees run to more than double those a solicitor would charge.

Alternatively, some banks do not go so far as to appoint themselves as executor, but pressurise the testator into appointing a professional executor such as the bank itself. In doing so it shrewdly fails to advise clients, who may be unaccustomed to dealing with Will issues, that they are perfectly entitled to choose whoever they wish to fulfil the role.

The Office of Fair Trading (OFT) investigated banks' fees and, having found that charges were being levied without the testator having full understanding of what was involved, requested that banks adhere to a more open policy in how it deals with Wills and the appointment of executors. There is now, in some cases, the possibility for a beneficiary to request that the bank's executor is replaced within four weeks after the testator's death, but you should be mindful that there is no legal obligation for the bank to stand down if it chooses not to. Moreover, your beneficiaries need to be aware of this short window of opportunity to change executors should they wish to.

It may be that you are content to appoint the bank to act as an executor. There is nothing wrong with that as long as you are made aware of the fees that will be charged on your estate when the time comes.

If you have already made your Will with a bank, check the small print and find out what your estate is likely to be charged.

So, what is the difference between using a bank and a law firm to draft your Will? Almost none. Most banks employ law firms to not only draft Wills on their behalf, but also to carry out the relevant Probate work when the time comes. The bank then pays the law firm a percentage of the takings and pockets the not insubstantial difference having attended to a minimal amount, if any, of the legalities.

Should you feel unhappy about the service you have received, banks have a complaints procedure through the Financial Ombudsman Service (FOS).

Key points to remember:

- Low or no Will-making fee but.....

- It is the most expensive way of administering your estate.

- Typically, banks charge around four to five percent (plus VAT) of the gross value of the estate for acting as the executor of your Will.

- There is the possibility that you will not be able to choose your own executors.

- If you have made your Will with a bank, it is worth checking to see whether it would be willing to renounce the role of executor now. Find out also what the charges would be for doing so.

- Remember, you can always make a new Will elsewhere which automatically revokes all previous Wills. It may sound drastic, but it could save your estate thousands of pounds.

- Banks are insured against mishandling your Will.

- There is a complaints procedure in place via the FOS.

◆

Did You Know?

Death taxes were introduced in the UK in 1796 in order to finance the war against the French.... We have been paying death taxes one way or another ever since.
Source: www.inheritanceissues.co.uk

◆

8

SOLICITORS

♦

According to a report conducted by the Office of Fair Trading, around 88 percent of people who make a Will in the UK choose to use a solicitor. A Legal Services Consumer Panel report on Will-writing (July 2011) suggests that the figure is around two thirds. Either way, it is small wonder that this is the most popular way to make a Will; solicitors are legally qualified, robustly regulated, and covered by insurance for the rare occasion when some form of recompense is required. In short, they appear to have all angles covered.

If you choose to engage with a solicitor, you are effectively paying for their time and their expertise. They are specialists in the field; they know the law. Most solicitors can split hairs for hours just for the joy of flexing their cerebral muscles so when it comes to Wills, those who specialise in the field should know all there is to know. And it is at this point that you need to ask questions about the decisions that you have come to. Are they sound? If your Will is controversial, what are the chances of it being successfully contested? Can the Bad Boy make life a misery for the Good Guy? How can you avoid paying IHT? Will the manner in which you have chosen to donate to charity cause any problems for your executors to administer? Are there any other factors to take into account that you have not thought of? All of these questions and more should be asked by you and then answered by your solicitor. This is the expertise that you are actually seeking and paying for, and it is why you are choosing to use a solicitor rather than any other Will-making avenue. Most solicitors will be happy to give you around 20 minutes of free time for an initial consultation. If your chosen firm is too busy to do this, then the chances are they will too busy to give you a good service. Fear not, there are plenty more that will.

As with most things in life, there is good and bad in all professions and solicitors are not excluded from this old adage. Some have a vocational calling to serve the public and develop that most crucial of things: a rich and successful working client/practitioner relationship. It is their driving force and, when it is present, it is immediately obvious to anyone who has dealings with them. If you find one, use them, forge links, give them all your business and recommend them to all and sundry, for they are diamonds.

Then there are others who, essentially, are business people with deadlines to meet and are target driven. Obviously there is nothing wrong with a healthy enterprising spirit except it does appear to compromise any humanitarian sentiment lurking within. The result is that such types rarely demonstrate awareness, or even having the vaguest inkling of how or why some of the public have a reluctance to shower business their way. If you encounter one of these, you may want to give them a wide berth for it is the portrayal of such indifference which greatly plays into the hands of the Will-writer, the banks and the DIY Will kit publishers.

If you have particularly complex family ties, a high value estate or highly structured assets, you will most likely need bespoke specialised advice from an experienced solicitor. But not all solicitors are equally qualified in all fields. Just as your local GP isn't qualified to perform brain surgery, your local high street solicitor may not be armed with the necessary experience to advise on every nuance of writing a multifaceted, complex Will. The best places to look for such an adviser are on the STEP website (for TEP qualified professionals) and in the Wills section of the Law Society website.

While on the subject of websites, for reasons known only to themselves, some law firms seem to be happy to bamboozle the lay public by listing issues surrounding Wills and Probate under the tag of Private Client, so, having tracked down a firm you wish to use, you may still have a hunt on your hands.

One of the most challenging aspects of making a Will with a solicitor is their apparent unwillingness to draw up Wills which are comprehensible to the lay person. Outmoded, arcane, legalistic jargon invariably means that the Will is so indecipherable that the testator rarely has a clue whether the instructions which have been stipulated have been correctly addressed. Solicitors will undoubtedly argue that the phrases and clauses used are well worn and proven to be watertight in the contestations of Wills. It is difficult, however, to believe that those within this most learned profession, some of whom can write with laser precision, cannot between them draft secure, intelligible Wills which are clear to the lay person. The upshot is twofold. Firstly, it ensures the exclusivity of Will writing: only the chosen few can understand and be employed to decipher it. Solicitors thus bat for themselves; they are, after all, businesses not charitable organisations. But more importantly, it means that a lay person, who purchases a Will from a solicitor employing such methods, can go to their grave without knowing whether their Will was correctly drafted at all. Proving otherwise after the event would be almost impossible for any executor or beneficiary. Such opaqueness should not occur at any level, let alone in relation to Wills given that it is a certainty that the testator will not be around to challenge the outcome. If you find a solicitor who has the resourcefulness to draft a Will in plain English, use them.

Fees

Solicitors' fees will vary depending on not only their experience and knowledge but also the complexity of your requirements. That said, not all people require a complex Will; for many a simple Will and some sound advice should suffice. Sadly, for all the legal requirement for openness and transparency, fees remain vague. Few law firms' websites give details of the costs for a simple Will or mirror Wills for couples. This is unfortunate as it would provide the reassurance many need to take the first steps towards using a law firm. Such failings create wariness and undoubtedly could be improved upon.

According to the Solicitors Regulation Authority (SRA), those within the profession have a duty to explain their fees clearly, explain if and when those fees are likely to change and also warn clients about other payments for which they may be responsible. This will be addressed in a Client Care letter but, sadly, only once you have engaged with the firm.

In the interest of completeness, it is worth noting the key findings of a 2011 Legal Services Consumer Panel report on the state of Will-writing in the UK. Whilst flaws in Will drafting were found, the chances are that few lay people would be able to notice the failings due to the outdated terminology used. Further still, without relaying yards of testimony, it concluded that there is significant room for improvement. One in four Wills written across the board by both solicitors and Will-writers were poorly drafted. However, the same report suggested that ninety percent of the lay public were happy with the service they received from using a solicitor. Obviously the efficacy of the Wills drafted remains unknown.

Key points to remember:

- Possibly the most expensive initial outlay is getting the Will drafted – but as with most things in life, you get what you pay for.

- Typically, solicitors charge anything from £120 + VAT for a single simple Will.

- Expect to pay significantly more if your Will and your estate is complicated.

- Some solicitors will offer home visits if required. Ask if you need this service.

- Not all solicitors have expertise in writing Wills or in handling complex trusts and estates so...

- Look out for those with TEP after their name.

- Solicitors must supply you with a Client Care letter to advise you of their fees.

- Do not give in to pressure to appoint a solicitor as an executor unless it suits you......

- You are legally entitled to choose your own executors.

- By using a solicitor, you will have been assessed for Testamentary Capacity which could prove to be invaluable.

- Solicitors are regulated under the Solicitors Regulation Authority and insured.

- Complaints can be made via the Legal Ombudsman.

◆

Did You Know?

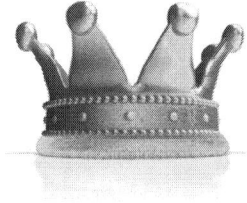

When a person dies intestate, without any known relatives, the estate goes to the Crown as Bona Vacantia ('ownerless goods'). Unclaimed estates are the subject of the BBC1 programme 'Heir Hunters'. Specialist Probate firms attempt to track down any living relatives to avoid the estate becoming the property of the Duchies of Cornwall and Lancaster.

♦

9

OTHER WILL PROVIDERS

♦

It seems everyone's at it. Open a magazine and the chances are it will, somewhere, be selling you their legal services. Search online for good impartial consumer advice, and you are thrust towards part of the website selling you a Will. Even the corner shop is at it.

There is now a growing trend for businesses which are not traditional legal establishments, to venture into the legal market. They trade on their recognisable brand name which is undeniably reputable and reassuringly familiar.

What these newbies appear to offer is, seemingly, a transparency to their fees which, in spite of all the legal requirements, few traditionals do. In order to garner business, overheads are lowered and costs are cut by employing trained consultants as opposed to qualified professionals. There is a minefield of difference between the two.

However, be cautious: these firms are not always cheaper, and the chances are they will not offer a better service but, due to familiarity of brand name and bullish marketing, they are trusted by the general public. Just because the brand is recognizable it does not mean that the legal service they are offering is of the same quality as other sectors they are involved in. They may even sell you a funeral in the process as they seem intent on pursuing a cradle to grave strategy.

Did You Know?

If military personnel die - even indirectly - as a result of injuries or diseases sustained while on military service, their estate is exempt from paying IHT. If this potentially applies to you, ensure your executors are aware of it.

◆

10

CHARITIES

◆

I f you are still pondering on the best way to go about making your Will, you may wish to avail yourself of the services of a solicitor and donate to charity at the same time; a win-win situation.

There are certain times of the year when solicitors run campaigns to incentivise us all into making a Will. These are periodically promoted both locally and nationally, depending on the type and location of the charity. The main thrust of these campaigns is that solicitors will draft the Will in return for a donation to the charity. In most cases, it is the solicitor who gives up his or her fee for the charity.

Here are just a couple of campaigns which are run regularly:

- Will Aid organises an annual campaign, usually in November, where participating solicitors can draw up a new Will, oversee an existing one, or even add a codicil (an amendment) to a Will. The Fee which the solicitor would have earned is directed towards the Will Aid pool for distribution amongst various chosen charities throughout the UK and worldwide.

- If you are over 55, Free Wills Month aims to generate income for various charities twice a year (March and

October) by asking you to leave a legacy in your Will to a participating charity. A simple Will can be made at participating solicitors – all of whom give their services free of charge. Each time a Free Will Month scheme runs, it is limited to certain chosen towns and cities and these usually change.

◆

11

WEIGHING IT ALL UP

◆

We've all done it. Bought something in a shop, got it home and been delighted with a hidden feature that proves to be worth its weight. Often this useful aspect is enough to turn the cost into a complete irrelevance such are its benefits, the level of enjoyment and satisfaction that it brings.

We've all been disappointed too. The purchase didn't quite hit the mark. Somehow there's a glitch which had not been anticipated and renders the purchase useless. It's not the end of the world if the item was bought in a pound shop; it is if you paid a king's ransom for it. In some cases, we have the opportunity to return the item and get a refund. In other cases, the whole experience gnaws away at us as we repent with monotonous regularity at the foolishness of our purchase.

As consumers, all purchases we make of any given product or service is the result of the perceived relationship between the cost, benefits and risks. The cost refers often as not to the financial outlay: how much did you have to fork out to buy it? The benefits refer to the product's features and what it will do for you, either by perception or in reality. Does it makes you feel good or is it useful? The risks are obvious: if it turns horribly sour, how bad could it actually be? So, the question we generally ask ourselves when buying a high end product or service is: do the features and branding justify the extra cost? Or could I get away with the cheaper version?

In the normal course of events, we quantify the merit of a purchase by weighing up the item's performance over a period of time, often boring everyone witless in the process particularly if gadgetry is involved. Making a Will is slightly different. In this instance you won't be able to see how your purchase performed, nor be around to offer your thoughts. Your loved ones will not have you to lean on and you can only surmise at how they will fare without you.

The temptation to over-simplify the complex Will-making ordeal in favour of the fastest, cheapest and least painful avenue may be difficult to resist, particularly in the current economic climate. But none of us know if the temporary-measure Will made with little attention to your whole, personal picture is the one that will one day be used. Is such a Will right for the people you leave behind? Is it worth the risk when the cost, in relation to the size of your estate, is barely discernible?   There are some things in life that are worth risking. This isn't one of them.

How bad could it actually be? The worst case scenario of your loved ones suffering months, if not years of stress, angst and confusion is really too hideous to consider. Believe me.

So find your diamond; it is the best thing you could wish for.

◆

12

CHOOSING YOUR EXECUTORS

♦

When you make your Will you will need to choose executors whose duty it will be to administer your estate and apply for the Grant of Probate from the Probate registry. The grant is a legal document which confirms that the executors have the legal right to administer the deceased's estate and are legally entitled to access the assets and distribute them to the beneficiaries in accordance with the Will. A Grant of Probate is required for all estates worth over five thousand pounds.

Most people choose two people they know well to act as their executors, but up to four is allowed; they may or may not be beneficiaries of the Will. Choosing a spouse as an executor is an obvious option but you should also choose alternative and substitute executors in case of situations where your spouse, for whatever reason, cannot act for you.

Either way, what is important is that your executors are trustworthy, morally sound, have both the personal and administrative skills to deal with the countless problems which can arise and who, most importantly, are happy to take on the responsibility. Equally important, and rarely commented upon, is the need for your executors to have some kind of rapport; there is little to be gained from appointing two people who find it impossible to agree on anything. There can be significant and sometimes difficult decisions to make surrounding your estate, so a meeting of minds is crucial.

The role can be particularly challenging. In contentious and difficult estates one becomes the bearer of bad news, walking the tricky tightrope between opposing beneficiaries. Without the luxury of impartiality a lay executor, who is potentially emotionally imbedded, can feel overwrought and overloaded with responsibility. Grieving for the loss of a loved one and making pivotal, irreversible decisions are not happy bed fellows.

However, one of the key advantages of choosing lay executors is that you are giving them the opportunity and the freedom, when the time comes, to apply for Probate themselves should they wish to, thereby saving the estate a lot of money in the process. There is a steady increase in the amount of lay, non-professional executors who are independently applying for Probate without the use of a solicitor at all. Whilst it may, on the face of it, appear to be a daunting task, if the estate is a relatively simple one it is unlikely to be difficult to administer. If it proves to be more complicated or time-consuming than first thought, your executors will be in the happy position of being able to seek assistance either from a law firm of their choice or a Probate broker.

Law firms

There is an increasing amount of law firms offering part administration of an estate, or merely the application for Grant of Probate. Anxious for business, there are deals to be done. Even the haughtiest of solicitors can bear more than a passing resemblance to a used-car salesman should circumstances dictate so, should they wish to take this route, your executors can hunt around for a number of quotes from rival law firms and, where necessary, negotiate an attractive fixed fee.

Probate brokers

Alternatively, your executors could use a relatively new service which has come to the fore: Probate brokers are businesses which deal in administering estates by undercutting the fees which banks and average law firms charge for applying for Grant of Probate and/or the administering of an estate. The brokers tender potential work out to a panel of chosen law firms and they, in turn, compete with each other by offering a keen and competitive fixed fee for the work thus reducing the administration fees for the estate. As the charges are fixed, there is the comfort of knowing what the end bill will be rather than the hourly rate which many solicitors prefer to charge.

According to a report prepared by the Office of Fair Trading, the public is wasting around £40 million a year by failing to shop around for quotes for Wills and executor services, and given that a report by the Legal Services Board found that only 11 percent of us bother to shop around for quotes at all, a Probate broker could save you the hassle. They are certainly worthy of consideration.

Solicitors as executors

For some testators appointing a professional executor, such as the bank or a solicitor, is a perfectly acceptable and logical path to take. They may not know anyone who would wish to take on the role or, if the Will is particularly complex, it may take considerable skill to administer the estate. Further still, if the Will is controversial, one of the key advantages of appointing a solicitor as an executor is that they should remain untouched by opposing factions within families and should be able to offer unbiased, objective, advice to all. A solicitor is also likely to be highly experienced in liquidating estates and should know all the procedures to recoup money due to the estate – not least from the taxman. Finally, and importantly, if you have appointed a solicitor as executor, he or she will be liable for any mistakes which are made during the course of settling the estate.

If you are considering appointing a professional executor, be it bank, Will-writer or solicitor, it is of paramount importance that you are advised of the charges which will be levied on your estate when the time comes. It is your right to know; it is a legal requirement. The most obvious way of ascertaining this is to quote the value of your estate, as calculated earlier, and ask for an indication of what the charges would be at today's rate for carrying out the role of executor in, say, the next six months. If the professional executor tactically avoids giving you a clear answer, find another firm to do business with.

One final word on appointing solicitors: if you are considering using both a lay executor such as a family member or friend, together with your solicitor as joint executors, it is worth mentioning that it is not unknown for solicitors to take a back seat and allow the lay executor to carry out the bulk of the administration, only for the solicitor to produce an invoice at the end for their meagre input. It would be nice to say this rarely happens, but it appears to be more common than one would care to hear.

If you have already made a Will:

If you have already made a Will it may be worth checking the paperwork to see whom you have appointed (either unsuspectingly or otherwise) as an executor. As mentioned earlier, some banks and Will-writers will fulfil the role of an executor by appointing themselves – it may be in the small print - so they will carry out the administration for a princely sum. If it isn't in the small print some banks, and less scrupulous solicitors, will apply undue pressure to ensure they are appointed. Unfortunately, it goes with the territory: the administration of the estate is the lucrative part of the Will industry.

If you made your Will some time ago and have chosen lay executors, consider too whether they are still suitable to carry out the task. Are they still mentally and physically fit? Are they geographically available or could it be that they are no longer suitable for other reasons.

You can always change your executors. You will, most likely, have to pay a small fee to make an alteration to your Will (a codicil) but it will be a paltry sum in comparison to the fees which will be incurred if a firm is involved in the administration of your Will.

Key points when choosing Executors:

- If you have already made your Will with a bank or a Will-writing firm, you may have appointed it to act as an executor. Check the small print. Banks will charge around five percent of the estate's gross value.

- Solicitors may quietly appoint themselves. Charges vary; typically around two percent plus VAT. However, some firms may use a mix of hourly rates, usually around £250 plus VAT together with a lower percentage of the estate; others leave an open ended bill and charge by the hour – which usually racks up the highest bill.

- Be aware that other fees may apply. Factors such as the number of beneficiaries in the Will, the amount of accounts the estate holds, whether there is IHT to pay and dealings with HMRC will all impinge on the end costs.

- Both the banks and solicitors can be an expensive way of administering your estate.

- The alternative is to choose two to four people you know. Ensure you choose substitute executors too.

- When the time comes your lay executors may wish to apply for Probate themselves.

- Alternatively, if it proves to be too complex or time consuming, they can seek out the best deal with a solicitor or a Probate broker. Fixed fees are nearly always the cheapest.

- Lay executors can only charge the estate for out of pocket expenses.

- According to the Office of Fair Trading, 43 percent of people who make a Will with a solicitor appoint them as an executor. Unfortunately, 23 percent of them were unaware of the firm's fees (OFT June 2010).

◆

We have attended to the legal aspects surrounding death. It is now time to look at the more personal and practical issues which will need to be addressed by your family and executors.

Some Will writing professionals may lack the personal touch required to administer the more intimate aspects surrounding the end of life, so it is important that you complete a Letter of Wishes for them stating your preferences.

If you are going to appoint lay executors it would be wise to complete a comprehensive version; it will assist them endlessly at a time when they will appreciate your assistance.

If you are unsure what a Letter of Wishes is... read on.

◆

Did You Know?

The longest known Will ever written was that of Englishwoman Frederica Evelyn Stilwell Cook. Granted Probate in 1925, it was 1,066 pages long, and had to be bound in four volumes; her estate was worth $100,000.

Source: Wikipedia

◆

13

Your Letter of Wishes

♦

Leaving a tidy estate generally revolves around two issues: making a Will, and writing a Letter of Wishes. We have already looked at your options for attending to the legal and financial aspects of dying but for some people it is the more personal matters that are equally, if not more, important. In spite of us living in materialistic and consumer driven times, sometimes it isn't all about the money.

A Letter of Wishes is a separate document to a Will which you complete in order to offer guidance about specific things that should happen after your death. Solicitors often use them in connection with Discretionary Trusts - then a Letter of Wishes becomes a guide to assist the trustee(s) on how the deceased would wish them to manage the trust's funds. Alternatively where children are involved, and guardians have been appointed, a Letter of Wishes may contain guidance on how the children should be raised in terms of, for example, their education and their religious upbringing.

However, not all people making Wills have either the wealth to set up trusts or indeed the need to appoint guardians, but everyone should write a Letter of Wishes. We should all pass on our wishes even if we have no intention of ever making a Will.

By writing your very personal Letter of Wishes, you have the opportunity to leave clear instructions and guidelines about the more practical and intimate matters which will need to be tackled when you die. These issues do not, as a rule, get dealt with in the Will-making process but, by addressing them now, you will assist your family and executors in tying up your estate efficiently and effectively in the future.

No matter what your religious persuasion there will one day, more than likely, be a funeral of sorts to commemorate your life. Most of us would wish to choose its format, regardless of whether the service is held in a church, a hut or a field. It is your right to indicate your preferences. For example, you may wish to advise on the type of funeral you would prefer; whether it is to be religious funeral, a civil ceremony or humanist service. You may also wish to choose the music and readings which are to be used and whether you wish to be buried or cremated. You are not expected to become fully conversant in all matters funereal but, by offering some simple guidelines for your executors, you will take away much of the guesswork and stress which can accompany death.

The chances are you have possessions. They may be expensive, state of the art gizmos or they may be simple, sentimental belongings which mean a great deal to you. There may be a house full of personal effects; there may be just a drawer full. Either way, you would probably wish to have a say in how these items are distributed after you die. As previously mentioned, you may want to include high value items in your Will as specific gifts but you can also pass on instructions as to who should receive your other, less costly, personal possessions. You may also wish to consider whether you would like any items to go to a charity.

It is important that you tell your family members if you have registered as an organ donor or whether you wish to donate your body to medical science. As time is of the essence in such matters, you should advise them now. All of these things, and more, can be addressed in a Letter of Wishes and in an ideal world, we should all give some thought to completing one.

Whilst these issues may appear to be seemingly innocuous they, and more, are so often the cause of family contention and angst for the bereaved. It is widely acknowledged by those professionals who deal with grieving families that confrontation and disagreements, often over what appear to be trifling issues, can all too often lead to litigation which destroys families. Anything that can be done to avert such misery should be tackled.

Writing your Letter of Wishes

If you have made your Will with a solicitor, some will offer a simple tick-list for you to complete as a Letter of Wishes. It will cover the basics such as preferences for your funeral and whether you wish to be buried or cremated. This may or may not suffice.

Some law firms supply their clients with a copy of *Last Orders, The Essential Guide to Your Letter of Wishes* which is a simple but comprehensive book which, once completed, serves as a Letter of Wishes as well as a guide.

The majority of solicitors will, however, do nothing; neither mentioning the pitfalls of neglecting to undertake the task nor bothering to flag up ways of averting family disputes that can potentially arise. Many are of the opinion that as a Letter of Wishes is not a legally binding document, it is outside their remit. It seems an interesting position to adopt, given that they appear content enough to draw up a Letter of Wishes in respect of a Discretionary Trust, presumably at a cost to the client. It is even more worrying that they appear uninterested in attempting to avert potential disputes and even litigation amongst families. Then again, why would they?

You may wish to produce your own document outlining your choices for the issues mentioned. Alternatively, you may wish to read and complete your own copy of *Last Orders*. Once completed correctly, it should save incalculable amounts of stress.

Online Letters of Wishes

In the interest of completeness, it is worth noting that there are now online facilities where you can store details of your life, your online accounts, assets and passwords as well as instructions for your funeral to assist your executors and family. This is a relatively new trend so the security of such services is yet to be determined. If all you are storing in a cloud is your funeral wishes, the chances are no computer geek would ever think it worth hacking into. If the information is more sensitive you may need to think again.

Unlike a Will, a Letter of Wishes is not a legal document, and therefore not legally binding. However, generally speaking, most families *want* to honour the wishes of the deceased; it can help them in their grieving process. You may also wish to bear in mind that, because they are not binding documents, executors and family member can overrule requests should circumstances dictate. You may ask: why bother completing a Letter of Wishes if executors have the power to ignore it? One could equally ask: why appoint executors who are likely to?

Once completed, your Letter of Wishes or copy of *Last Orders* can be altered as often as you need to. Wishes change over time so you should reassess your choices periodically. It is important that you advise your executors where your wishes can be found when the time comes and whether you would prefer its content to remain confidential.

None of us know the moment when our Letter of Wishes will be needed but by leaving clear answers and passing on key information you will have contributed greatly to making your passing as peaceful as possible for those remaining.

◆

Did You Know?

Age isn't a barrier to being an organ donor. The oldest donor was 84, and the oldest recipient 85. One organ donor can help up to nine people.
Source: NHS Blood and Transplant 2012

◆

Human bodies are used to teach students about the structure of the body and how it works. They are also used to train and develop the skills of surgeons and pathologists.
Source: Human Tissue Authority

Contact details for organ, body and tissue donation are at the back of the book.

.◆

14

BUYER BEWARE

◆

Wills and Probate are specialised areas. Making sense of the information that is bandied around can be confusing for anyone who is unfamiliar with the jargon, the financial implications or the administration of an estate. Many websites, articles, advertisements and leaflets are worded in such a way as to confuse, create uncertainty and, it has to be said, play on the public's fears which transfers into them making poor, uninformed decisions and purchasing services which they may not need at all.

Astute attention to the wording used is needed to sift through the clever scaremongering phrases that are used to sell services. Take this example of two very reputable magazines and how they each dealt with the same issue of applications for Probate:

A. In its January 2012 edition, Magazine 1 stated that according to its "own research 90% of people use solicitors when applying for Probate". The magazine went on to state that "most solicitors charge up to five percent of the estate's value" and, having scared the reader witless, went on to offer its own Legal Services.

B. In May 2012, Magazine 2 printed an article which started with the headline "Solicitors Lose Probate Market Share", quoted the 2011 data from the Probate Service (a division of HM Courts and Tribunals Services) and revealed that "56% of grants (of Probate) went to private individuals without approaching solicitors" at all.

The first magazine quoted statistics which were based on its "own research". The second magazine's statistics were figures direct from an independent, reputable source.

The first magazine was SAGA.
The second The Law Society Gazette.
Most solicitors charge around two percent of the estate's value.

◆

15

STORING YOUR WILL

◆

Having made your Will, what should you do with it? In the UK, there is no requirement to register a Will which increases the chance of it being lost, destroyed or never discovered. Given that your Will is one of the most important documents you will ever sign, it is crucial that you take care to safeguard it and ensure it will be found by your executors when the time comes. If for any reason it isn't, your estate will be distributed as if your Will never existed.

The business of storing Wills can be a lucrative for those involved. An annual fee is charged for its safe keeping and, over several years, can prove to be costly for the consumer and a retirement pension plan for the provider. Sadly, there is often no guarantee that the Will has been safely stored at all so it is particularly important that you are cautious where, and with whom, you choose to store yours. It is not unheard of for fly-by-night Will-writers to go out of business and the Will storage, for which clients have paid, amounts to the local skip.

If you have chosen to write a DIY Will, there are additional risks involved. Remember, there will be no professional to verify that the DIY Will was ever completed and there is just a single copy of it. Therefore, there is a greater chance of it going undiscovered, it being destroyed either mistakenly or intentionally, or even the possibility of forgery, so it is particularly important that you keep it somewhere safe and advise your executors where they can find it. If you are worried about the possibility of underhanded behaviour at all, a DIY Will is probably not suitable for you and it would be advisable to seek an alternative Will making option or, at very least, ensure you store it safely in any of the options below.

Some of the many Will storage alternatives:

- If you have made your Will via a Will-writer, the firm will most likely store it for you for an annual fee. This is usually around £20 - £40 which, over a period of time, can mount up. Ensure you know the registered location of it.

- The Ministry of Justice will store your Will for a one-off fee of just £20. You can deposit your Will and any codicil at the same time, in the same envelope, and the fee is still just £20. You will need a safe custody Will envelope pack, which can be obtained from the District Probate Registry or the Record Keepers Department.

- Your bank will store your Will for you for a small fee – generally around £15 - £25 annually. However be careful! If the testator places the original Will in a safety deposit box in a bank, when he or she dies, the box cannot be opened until Probate has been granted but Probate cannot be granted without the original Will!

- Alternatively, your bank may offer to hold your Will for you free of charge. The costly condition is that you appoint it as an executor. *(To be avoided if possible.)*

- Which? the one-time consumer champion now has a Legal Service which is allied to a company call Lifetime Legal, which will store your Will and any other documents you wish for a one off fee of £60.

- If you have made your Will via a solicitor they will, most likely, keep the original (or sometimes a copy) in a strong room. Many offer this facility free of any charge for as long as you wish; others charge a small one-off fee. As well as storing the Will they may, potentially, register it elsewhere too.

- Many solicitors use a company called Certainty to register the Will for a one-off fee of £25 plus VAT. This facility is also open to the public. Certainty also offers a Will tracing service.

- If a law firm closes down, you will need to locate your Will. This can be done via the Law Society.

- You can keep your Will at home but it is crucial it remains safe and in a waterproof and fireproof place.

- In all cases, ensure you tell your executors where your Will is lodged.

The list above is not exhaustive but just a sample of the wide range of options which are available. This, in itself, demonstrates how easily a Will can go undetected. Consider then, how your executors will track down your Will.

Ensure your Will can be found!

◆

Did You Know?

The shortest Will in the world is recorded as being just two words long: "Vse zene", Czech for "all to wife". It was written on the bedroom wall of a man who realized his imminent demise and made a swift attempt to distribute his chattels before expiring.
Source: Wikipedia

◆

16

OTHER MATTERS TO CONSIDER

♦

Noone of us like to dwell on end-of-life issues but it may be useful to consider some of the other matters you may wish to put in place. This is not the book for an in-depth discussion of such issues, but your solicitor or Will-writer may advise you to do any or all of the following:

- Trusts are generally put in place either during the lifetime of, or after the death of, a testator. Put very simply, it is a way of locking away and protecting assets. Trusts are often used to safeguard money for children, charities, in order to avoid paying care home fees, and for many other reasons. They can even be seen as an effective way of avoiding Inheritance Tax or hoodwinking the State benefits system and, if done properly, is all completely legal.

- Lasting Powers of Attorney (LPAs) are legal documents which allow you to appoint someone you trust to take care of you and/or your finances in the event that you lack the mental capacity to do so. LPAs replaced Enduring Powers of Attorney (EPAs) in October 2007. Those who have EPAs which were made before that date can continue to use them although new EPAs cannot be created.

There are two types of LPAs:

- Health and Welfare
- Property and Financial affairs

Solicitors can be employed to apply to register these at a cost of around £500 plus VAT for each LPA, some Will-writers offer the service for around £300. Alternatively, you can apply for this yourself should you wish to. Details, step-by-step instructions and downloadable forms are available from the Ministry of Justice. It currently costs £130 to register each LPA with the Office of the Public Guardian. Details are at the back of the book.
Note: an LPA cannot be used until it is registered.

- You may also wish to consider an Advance Decision, formerly known as a Living Will, in which you can detail the medical treatment you would prefer not to receive in order to sustain life. Again, you should consult a solicitor and your doctor before you make such a decision.

◆

17

WHEN TO REVIEW YOUR WILL

◆

Whichever way you choose to make your Will, it is important that you review it from time to time to ensure that its content remains relevant. It is recommended that this is done around every five years. However, there are other factors which should prompt a review regardless of the time frame. The following list is not exhaustive but represents the more obvious suggestions:

- You marry or re-marry. Marriage automatically revokes or annuls a Will.

- You enter into a civil partnership. As with marriage, it automatically revokes a Will.

- You separate from your spouse or civil partner.

- You divorce *(Divorce partially revokes a Will)*.

- You gain a step child or adopt a child.

- Your financial circumstances change considerably for the better of worse.

- You have cash (pecuniary) legacies in your Will, the value of which will diminish over a period of time as a result of inflation. You may wish to review these regularly if they are not index-linked.

- One of the beneficiaries of the Will dies.

- You sell property or land which has been specified in your Will.

- You need to appoint a new executor: one or both is/are no longer suitable; for example, because of poor health, geographical relocation or death.

◆

18

TWELVE THINGS TO DO

◆

So, hopefully you have digested the content of this short book. The aim is to assist you in making some good, informed decisions which will ultimately support you and your loved ones. It would be easy to shelve the writing of your Will now, perhaps even postponing the task it indefinitely, but having come this far, here is a simple list of To Dos to help ensure that doesn't happen:

1. Make a list of your assets and subtract your debts to estimate the value of your estate. Even if you have already made a Will, it would be useful to know this figure.

2. If your estate is likely to be subject to Inheritance Tax, seek professional advice to see if you can reduce or avoid it.

3. Decide how you would like your estate to be distributed when the time comes. Consider your Will as if it could be needed in the next six months. If you have already made your Will, consider: does it need to be updated? Check Chapter 17.

4. Consider too, if you have valuable belongings and/or pets whether you would like to include them in your Will.

5. Make a list of your beneficiaries noting full names, addresses

with postcodes.

6. If you plan to donate to charity, note the charities' names, addresses and charity numbers.

7. Consider who you wish to appoint as executors. Ask them if they would like to fulfil the role. Ensure you choose substitute executors too. If you have already made your Will, check to see who you have appointed. Are they still suitable? If you have appointed a professional executor such as your bank, solicitor or Will-writer, find out how much the administration of the estate is going to cost.

8. Look for some price comparisons for making a Will. Ensure you compare like with like.

9. If you have made your Will with a solicitor, they will most likely, store it. If you have made it elsewhere, ensure you know its location. If you are going to keep the Will yourself, consider how and where you will safeguard it.

10. Write your Letter of Wishes.

11. Tell your executors where your Will is lodged and where you have placed your Letter of Wishes.

12. Review all the above periodically or when there are changes outlined in Section 11.

◆

Glossary of Terms

Administrator: The name given to a personal representative appointed by the court to oversee the administration of the deceased's estate where there is no valid Will. The Administrator will normally have to obtain Letters of Administration to show that he/she is the person with the legal authority to deal with the deceased's property.

Assets: Property, finances or other items of value owned by the deceased.

Beneficiary: A person who inherits under a Will.

Bequest: A gift of a particular object or cash left to somebody in a Will.

Chattels: Personal possessions (such as furniture, wine, pictures, jewellery, books, cars, etc) which are not used for business.

Child: Child of whatever age including illegitimate and adopted children. Step children are excluded unless specifically included in a Will.

Civil partner: A partner in a same sex relationship which has been registered and recognised by the Civil Partnership Act of 2004.

Codicil: A supplementary document which adds to or amends an existing Will by either modifying or revoking part of the existing Will. The codicil must be signed and witnessed, but the witnesses need not be the same as the original witnesses of the Will.

Co-executor: An executor who is appointed to act alongside another executor.

Co-habitee: Unmarried people who live together as man and wife or partners.

Deceased: The person who has died.

Discretionary trust: A trust under which funds are allocated among named potential beneficiaries at the discretion of the trustee(s).

Enduring Power of Attorney: A document that authorises someone to act on another's behalf. EPAs were replaced in 2007 by Lasting Powers of Attorneys (LPA). Existing EPAs remain valid unless cancelled by the maker.

Estate: All the assets and property of the deceased, to include (for example) property, vehicles, art, money, personal belongings and investments at the time of death.

Executor: The person appointed by a valid Will or Codicil to carry out its provision after death of the testator. The Executor usually has to apply for Probate of the Will to prove that he/she is the person with the legal authority to deal with the deceased's estate. A female Executor is referred to as an Executrix.

Grant of Letters of Administration: The document issued by the Probate Registry which confirms the right of an administrator to administer the estate of a person who has died intestate (or who has died with a valid will, but in circumstances where there is no executor willing or able to act).

Grant of Probate: The document issued by the Probate Registry to the executors of a Will, giving authorisation to the executors to administer the estate. If the deceased died intestate, the document will be a Grant of Letters of Administration.

Grant of Representation: The document issued by the Probate Registry which gives legal authority to deal with matters relating to someone who has died.

Guardian: A person who would be legally entrusted to manage the affairs of, or look after, the minor children in the event of the death of parents.

Inheritance Tax (IHT): A tax which is payable to the Government when the total estate of the deceased person exceeds the set threshold after debts have been paid. See the current Rates and Allowances for IHT on HMRC website: www.hmrc.gov.uk

Insolvent: A situation in which the liabilities of the deceased exceeds the value of the deceased's assets.

Intestate: A person who dies without making any (or any legally valid) Will. The estate will pass in accordance with the Intestacy Rules.

Issue: Children and all generations arising from them – grandchildren, great-grandchildren, etc.

Joint Tenancy: When a property is owned in joint names. When one of the partners die, the ownership of the property will pass directly to the surviving partner under the rules of survivorship.

Lasting Power of Attorney: A legal document enabling appointed attorney(s) to make decisions on your behalf. There are two types: financial and health.

Lawyer: A term for someone who is qualified as a solicitor or barrister.

Legacy: A gift or bequest left in a Will or a codicil.

Letter of Wishes: A non-legal, non binding document to accompany a Will which guides executors about specific things that should happen after death.

Life interest: A gift which permits the right to income from an asset or the right to reside in a property for the duration of the beneficiary's life, after which the asset or property passes to another named person.

Minor: A person under the age of 18.

Next of kin: The closest relative who would be entitled to the estate if a person died intestate.

Paralegal: Someone who undertakes legal administrative support work but who is not a qualified solicitor.

Pecuniary legacy: A bequest which is a set amount of money, decided at the time you write your Will. Its real value will decrease over time unless it is expressly linked to the Retail Price Index.

Personal Representative(s): The executor(s) or administrator(s) of an estate. If there is more than one personal representative, they must work together to decide matters between them. Disagreements between personal representatives can cause expensive delays.

Probate: The document issued by the Probate Registry after a death, confirming that the deceased's Will is valid and authorising the Executors to administer the estate.

Probate Registry: The Government office which deals with Probate matters. The Principal Probate Registry is situated in London, with district offices in other parts of the country.

Residue legacy: The remainder of an estate left after all funeral and legal expenses, IHT, debts, liabilities and pecuniary legacies have been paid.

Revoke: Cancel retrospectively.

Solicitor: A qualified and regulated legal professional who is regulated by the Solicitors Regulation Authority.

Solvent: When the value of the deceased's assets exceeds any liabilities of the deceased.

Specific bequests: Detailed items gifted in the Will. These may be referred to as 'specific legacies' or in the case of gifts of money 'pecuniary legacies'.

Spouse: The person to whom a person is legally married.

STEP: The Society of Trust and Estate Practitioners. A worldwide organisation whose members provide expert advice on the law and tax rules surrounding trusts, estates and inheritance.

Tenants in Common: When each within a partnership owns a set portion of a property or land. On the death of one of the owners, their share will pass to the beneficiaries of their Will or be distributed under the rules of intestacy if no Will has been made.

Testamentary Capacity: The legal term used to describe a person's legal and mental ability to make or alter a valid Will.

Testator: A male who has made a legally valid Will. A female Testator is called a Testatrix.

Trust: Either created in a testator's lifetime or included in, or as part of, a Will. Often used to protect and control assets after death. Can be used, for example, to ensure children are catered for, disabled children are taken care of or as a means of avoiding Inheritance Tax.

Trustee: The person given the legal authority to administer a Trust.

Will: A witnessed document in which the maker (the testator) sets out what is to happen to his or her estate after he or she dies.

◆

Useful Addresses

Bona Vacantia
Treasury Solicitor's Office (BV) One Kemble Street,
London WC2B 4TS
Tel: 020 7210 4700
www.bonavacantia.gov.uk

Certainty Will Registry
The Chapel, Chapel Lane, Lapworth, Warwickshire, B94 6EU
Tel: 0845 408 0404
www.certainty.co.uk

Cinnamon Trust
10 Market Square, Hayle, Cornwall, TR27 4HE
Tel: 01736 757 900
www.cinnamon.org.uk

Estate Planning Arbitration Scheme
IDRS Limited, International Dispute Resolution Centre,
70 Fleet Street, London, EC4Y 1EU
Tel: 020 7520 3800
www.idrs.ltd.uk

Free Wills Month
www.freewillsmonth.org.uk

Financial Ombudsman Service
South Quay Plaza, 183 Marsh Wall, London, E14 9SR
Tel: 0800 023 4567 and 020 7964 0500
www.financial-ombudsman.org.uk

Financial Services Authority
25 The North Colonnade, Canary Wharf, London E14 5HS
Tel: 0845 606 1234
www.fsa.gov.uk

Human Tissue Authority
151 Buckingham Palace Road, Victoria, London, SW1W 9SZ
Tel: 020 7269 1999
www.hta.gov.uk

Institute of Professional Will Writers
Trinity Point, New Road, Halesowen, West Midlands B63 3HY
Tel: 0345 257 2570
www.ipw.org.uk

The Law Society of England & Wales
The Law Society's Hall, 113 Chancery Lane, London WC2A 1PL
Tel: 020 7242 1222
www.lawsociety.org.uk

Legal Ombudsman
PO Box 6806, Wolverhampton, WV1 9WJ.
Tel: 0300 555 0333
www.legalombudsman.org.uk

Ministry of Justice (Lasting Power of Attorney Forms)
Tel: 0300 456 0300
www.justice.gov.uk/forms/opg/lasting-power-of-attorney

Ministry of Justice (Will storage)
Record Keeper's Dept, Principal Registry of the Family Division,
First Avenue House, 42 - 49 High Holborn, London WC1V 6NP
Tel: 020 7947 7022
www.justice.gov.uk

My Lost Account (Website)
www.mylostaccount.org.uk

My Lost Account (British Bankers' Association)
Lost Accounts Manager, The British Bankers' Association,
Pinners Hall, 105-108 Old Broad Street, London EC2N 1EX
Tel: 020 7216 8909

My Lost Account (Building Societies Association)
Lost Savings, The Building Societies Association,
6th Floor, York House,
23 Kingsway, London WC2B 6UJ
Tel: 020 7520 5900

My Lost Account (National Savings and Investments)
Tracing Service, National Savings and Investments,
Blackpool FY3 9YP
Tel: 0500 007 007

Office of Fair Trading
Fleetbank House, 2-6 Salisbury Square, London EC4Y 8JX
Tel: 020 7211 8000
www.oft.gov.uk

Office of the Public Guardian
PO Box 18165, Birmingham, B2 2WH

Organ Donation
NHS Blood and Transplant,
Organ Donation & Transplantation Directorate,
Fox Den Road, Stoke Gifford, BRISTOL, BS34 8RR
Tel: 0300 123 2323
www.organdonation.nhs.uk

Probate Brokers
Final Duties Ltd, Second Floor Office Suite, Marlin,
459 London Road, Camberley, Surrey GU15 3JA
Tel: 0800 731 8722
www.finalduties.co.uk
Other Probate Brokers are available

RSPCA Pet For Life
Wilberforce Way, Southwater, Horsham, West Sussex RH13 9RS
Tel: 0300 123 0239
www.homeforlife.org.uk

Society of Trust & Estate Practitioners (STEP)
Artillery House (South)
11 - 19 Artillery Row, London, SW1P 1RT
Tel: 020 7340 0500
www.step.org

Solicitors Regulation Authority (SRA)
The Cube, 199 Wharfside Street, Birmingham, B1 1RN
Tel: 0870 606 2577 and 0121 329 6800
www.sra.org.uk

Society of Will Writers
Newland House, Weaver Road, Lincoln, LN6 3QN.
Tel: 01522 687888
www.willwriters.com

Will Aid
Roundham House, Oxen Road, Crewkerne, Somerset, TA18 7HN
Tel: 01460 271178,
www.willaid.org.uk

◆

Also by Patricia C Byron

LAST ORDERS

The Essential Guide to Your Letter of Wishes

This is a book intended to assist anyone and everyone. It deals with that perennial taboo, the subject of death. It is not a Will, nor should it be considered as such. It is, however, the essential guide to producing your Letter of Wishes which, once completed correctly, should save incalculable amounts of stress to those you leave behind and take most, if not all, of the guesswork out of the administration of your estate. It will offer a vast amount of helpful information about whom your executors should contact, the funeral you would wish for, your finances, your belongings, and even your pets.

This book is simple yet comprehensive
Its usefulness cannot be overstated

You may not feel you need such a book, but consider this scenario: imagine your child, sibling, or friend is executor to your will. When the sad time comes to wind up your estate, where would they start?

Would they be able, for example, to answer the following questions:

- Who do you wish to have informed of your passing?
- Is there a family cemetery plot?
- If so, where is the paperwork to support that?
- Where are the deeds to your house?
- Where is your Will?
- Have you registered as an organ donor?

- Who has spare sets of keys to your house?
- Who knows the code to your burglar alarm?
- Does your home have a safe?
- Who is to take care of your pet poodle Pandora?
- Equally important, who do you not want to take care of Pandora?

There are over 100 simple but pertinent questions which need to be answered by you in Last Orders. Those answers will eradicate doubt and offer clarity for the executors of your Will and those you leave behind. Such issues rarely get addressed in the Will-making process but are invariably the issues which families fall out over.

In researching Last Orders, the author consulted with solicitors, funeral directors, the Society of Trust & Estate Practitioners, The Law Society, MENCAP, but perhaps most telling of all, is that she has personal knowledge and experience of administering estates.

Since its launch in April 2010, and following the author being interviewed on the BBC's Radio 4 Woman's Hour, Last Orders sold out and went to reprint. It has since become a staple item for those wishing to put their affairs in order. Along with the general public, there are now law firms within the UK Legal 500 using Last Orders for their Will-making clients as well as members of the Society of Trusts and Estate Practitioners, estate planners, chartered accountants and independent financial advisors.

Available from:
www.lastorders.org
www.stellarstore.co.uk
Amazon, Waterstone's and all good bookshops.

◆

LAST ORDERS

The Essential Guide to Your Letter of Wishes

"One of the intended consequences of Last Orders is to prompt the reader to discuss the issues raised and their wishes with their family and friends. I hope the author appreciates just how valuable this is at heading off potential post-death arguments and perhaps even avoiding costly litigation. The writer (of this review) would wholeheartedly recommend this book for both clients and practitioners alike."
The Law Society Gazette

"The detailed guidelines and checklists represent an indispensible aid to anyone who has to tackle the affairs of a loved one especially at a time of grief. For the executor, it will be a tremendous time saving exercise..."
The Society of Trust & Estate Practitioners Journal

"For guidance on making end of life provision, we particularly like the book Last Orders, by Patricia C Byron...."
Good Housekeeping

"Last Orders is a very practical guide to death, and deals with all of the issues relating to all the aspects in your life that need to be addressed by your loved ones when you die. Would my epitaph be "Sorry you missed the Deadline"?"
Manchester Law Society's Messenger

"..the modest cost will be one of your best investments.."
Archibald, Campbell & Harley, Solicitors, Edinburgh"

"A splendid little book which steers a person through the essentials for the recording of information and expressing wishes, to friends and executors when the person dies."
SB Consulting, Chartered Tax Advisors, London

"Almost anyone will find this guide helpful in ensuring their explicit wishes after death are committed to paper...while family members or friends have lots of information and support."
Cancer Nursing Practice

"Last Orders is certainly a valid and useful book which could assist us all in leaving clear and unambiguous instructions about our final wishes."
Berkshire Life

"This book is, quite simply, exceptionally useful."
Great British Life Website

◆

About The Author

When Patricia C Byron was hit by a tsunami of events she had to deal with the deaths of three of the closest people in her life. Arranging funerals, tidying up estates and emptying houses, all gave her much cause and time for deep contemplation. In her grief, she reflected on how death could be handled in a way which assisted the bereaved as well as enhancing how the deceased would be remembered.

She had written the bones of her book, *Last Orders,* for a friend who was terminally ill and published it in 2010 without any agenda other than to assist the public in an area where few had ventured. The book's relative success and acclaim has paved the way for it currently being used by top tier law firms as well as financial advisors, estate planners and those members of the public who wish to get their affairs in order.

She now writes articles on end of life issues from a lay perspective for a law based website, LawSkills, and offers presentations on the importance of leaving a good legacy. She is not a lawyer, a Will-writer or a banker.

◆